Earth's Path

my world of science

Published in the United States of America by Cherry Lake Publishing
Ann Arbor, Michigan
www.cherrylakepublishing.com

Reading Adviser: Marla Conn MS, Ed., Literacy specialist, Read-Ability, Inc.
Content Adviser: Brittany Burchard M.Ed., Science teacher
Book Design: Jennifer Wahi
Illustrator: Jeff Bane

Photo Credits: ©Artsplav/Shutterstock, 5; ©Vladimir Ivanovski/Shutterstock, 7; ©cigdem/Shutterstock, 9; ©Robert Kneschke/Shutterstock, 11; ©Tong_stocker/Shutterstock, 13; ©carlosobriganti/Shutterstock, 15; ©Sushitsky Sergey/Shutterstock, 17; ©Teguh Mujiono/Shutterstock, 19; ©Matic Stojs/Shutterstock, 21; ©Johan Swanepoel/Shutterstock, 23; Cover, 10, 14, 16, Jeff Bane

Library of Congress Cataloging-in-Publication Data

Names: Marsico, Katie, author. | Bane, Jeff, 1957- illustrator.
Title: Earth's path / by Katie Marsico ; [illustrator] Jeff Bane.
Description: Ann Arbor, Michigan : Cherry Lake Publishing, [2018] | Series:
    My world of science | Audience: K to grade 3. | Includes bibliographical
    references and index.
Identifiers: LCCN 2018003268| ISBN 9781534128934 (hardcover) | ISBN
    9781534132139 (pbk.) | ISBN 9781534130630 (pdf) | ISBN 9781534133839
    (hosted ebook)
Subjects: LCSH: Earth (Planet)--Juvenile literature. | Earth
    (Planet)--Rotation--Juvenile literature. | Earth (Planet)--Orbit--Juvenile
    literature.
Classification: LCC QB631.4 .M366 2018 | DDC 525--dc23
LC record available at https://lccn.loc.gov/2018003268

Printed in the United States of America
Corporate Graphics

table of contents

About the author: Katie Marsico is the author of more than 200 reference books for children and young adults. She lives with her husband and six children near Chicago, Illinois.

About the illustrator: Jeff Bane and his two business partners own a studio along the American River in Folsom, California, home of the 1849 Gold Rush. When Jeff's not sketching or illustrating for clients, he's either swimming or kayaking in the river to relax.

Earth is one of eight **planets**.

Planets move in two ways.
One way is by **rotation**.

Earth rotates in 24 hours.

Some parts of Earth face the sun. Others don't.

This makes day and night.

Planets also **revolve**.
They revolve around the sun.

Each planet has its own **orbit**.
Orbits are shaped like **ovals**.

What other things are shaped like ovals?

Earth's orbit takes 365 days.

So Earth travels around the sun in one year.

Earth rotates while in orbit.

Earth is tipped to one side when it rotates.

Parts of Earth face
the sun's strongest
rays.

There is more daylight.
It is warmer.

Other parts face away
from strong rays.

There is less daylight.

It is cooler.

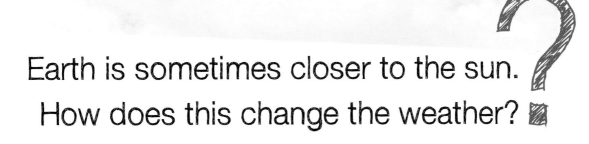

Earth is sometimes closer to the sun.
How does this change the weather?

Parts of Earth take turns facing the sun.

This makes the **seasons**. There are four seasons in one year.

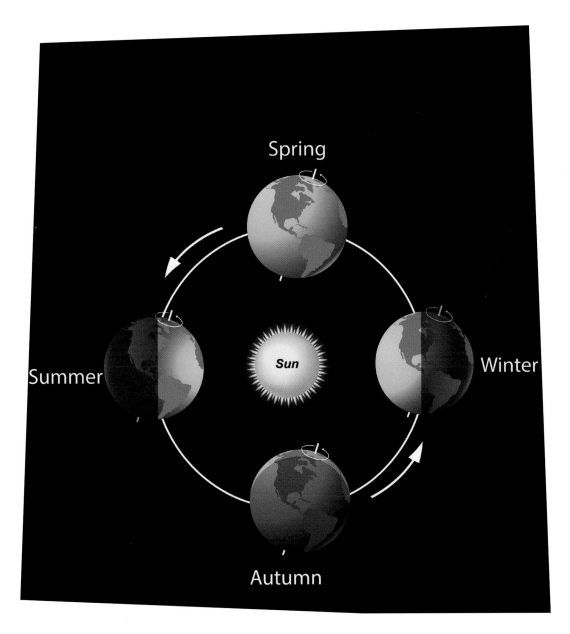

Spring

Summer

Sun

Winter

Autumn

The seasons are winter, spring, summer, and fall.

Each has different weather. Each has different amounts of daylight.

What is your favorite season?

Some **scientists** study Earth's path. They ask questions. They look for answers.

What would you like to study next?

glossary

orbit (OR-bit) curved path around the sun

ovals (OH-vuhlz) shapes like eggs

planets (PLAN-its) round objects in space that move in a path around the sun

revolve (rih-VAHLV-ing) to keep on turning in a circle around an object

rotation (roh-TAY-shuhn) the action of turning around a central point

scientists (SYE-uhn-tists) people who study nature and the world we live in

seasons (SEE-zuhnz) the four times of year known for certain weather and hours of daylight

index